EUROPEAN STEAM
IN THE 1970s

Paul Bryson

AMBERLEY

First published 2019

Amberley Publishing
The Hill, Stroud
Gloucestershire, GL5 4EP

www.amberley-books.com

Copyright © Paul Bryson, 2019

The right of Paul Bryson to be identified as
the Author of this work has been asserted in
accordance with the Copyrights, Designs and
Patents Act 1988.

ISBN 978 1 4456 9348 4 (print)
ISBN 978 1 4456 9349 1 (ebook)

British Library Cataloguing in Publication Data.
A catalogue record for this book is available from
the British Library.

Typesetting by Aura Technology and Software
Services, India. Printed in the UK.

Last Days of Steam in Western Europe

The rapid disappearance of steam from British Railways in the late 1960s was a bitter blow for the thousands of railway enthusiasts who had been brought up with the sounds, smells and sheer excitement of steam power. The industrial railways of Britain – the National Coal Board, Central Electricity Generating Board, British Steel and many more minor industrial concerns – continued to provide a smaller-scale outlet for some. But for those intent on experiencing main line steam, it was necessary to make a short trip to the Continent, where steam persisted throughout much of the 1970s and even into the 1980s.

In the West, from northern Portugal to eastern Austria, and everywhere in between, steam locomotives of all kinds could still be found on both passenger and freight workings of the State railways. This book illustrates some of the final steam locomotives working the main lines of Portugal, Spain, France, Italy, Austria and Germany.

In Portugal, on the lines around Porto and the Douro Valley in the north, a fascinating array of locomotives could be found. British-built broad gauge engines from the nineteenth century mixed with metre gauge Mallets throughout this region, which was widely regarded as a living museum at the time.

The broad gauge lines of Spain were home to some of the largest surviving steam engines in Europe. Although the mighty Garratts were withdrawn in 1971, immense 4-8-4s and 4-8-2s soldiered on before finally giving way to the standard 141F class 'Mikados' which hauled both passenger and freight until the mid-1970s. Major narrow gauge industrial lines at Ponferrada and Rio Tinto were also a mecca for rail enthusiasts.

In Italy, the ageing fleet of steam locos, most built in the early twentieth century, was mainly concentrated in the north of the country. Hundreds of locomotives were in use every day, with the lines radiating out from Milan being particularly busy.

Thousands of locos remained in service in West Germany at the beginning of the 1970s and on sheds in the Ruhr one could often find over fifty locos in steam. Old Prussian tank and tender engines worked alongside the ubiquitous 2-10-0 'Kriegsloks' and one could still see 'Pacific' class steam expresses hauling 500-ton trains on 'mile a minute' schedules.

Several hundred steam locomotives survived into the 1970s in Austria. Although half of the stock was made up of German 'Kriegsloks', a variety of classes of tank engines could be found hauling suburban services in the capital city of Vienna, crossing the plains of Bohemia and hauling heavy freight in spectacular mountain scenery.

In France, sadly, by the time of this author's first trip in 1972, little remained. Rusting steam locomotives could be found dumped throughout the country and although SNCF held many steam locomotives in reserve until the mid-1970s, workings were few and far between.

In Eastern Europe steam lasted well into the 1980s and beyond, though the political situation there rendered their pursuit more hazardous. Nevertheless, I was able to capture a few cross-border workings from East Germany, Czechoslovakia and Yugoslavia.

Portugal

Porto Boa Vista shed and works served the Porto metre gauge system of the Portuguese Railways (CP). Here, in August 1972, from left to right are three Kessler 2-6-0T tanks: CP No. E83, built in 1886; CP No. E102, built in 1907; and CP No. E114, built in 1908. Even when the photo was taken, the youngest engine was sixty-four years old!

It's hard to believe this metre gauge Kessler 2-6-0T, CP No. E83, built in 1886, pictured at Porto Boa Vista shed in August 1972, had been running around Porto for eighty-six years. Six engines of this class were still active in 1972.

Almost identical to its older classmates, this later metre gauge 2-6-0T is CP No. E114, built by Kessler in 1908 and pictured here on shed at Porto Boa Vista in August 1972.

Henschel 0-4-4-0T Mallet CP No. E167, built in 1908, at Porto Boa Vista shed, August 1972. Ten of these engines were based at Boa Vista for working the intensive service out of Porto Trindade.

Boa Vista served local trains from Porto Trindade to Senhora, Povoa de Varzim, Familcao and Fafe. Here, another of the Henschel 0-4-4-0T Mallets, CP No. E168, built in 1908, is seen at Porto Trindade in August 1972.

Henschel metre gauge 2-8-2T CP No. E144, built in 1931, departing Povoa de Varzim with a train for Porto in August 1972. These were the last class of steam engines built for the Portuguese metre gauge.

Contumil was the main broad gauge depot for the north of Portugal but was only opened in 1965, when the extension of Porto Campanha station forced the demolition of the old steam roundhouse at Campanha. At the time of my visit, on 7 August 1972, there were over twenty engines in steam and a further eight stored out of use.

CP broad gauge two-cylinder 2-8-0 No. 710, built by Schwartzkopf in 1913, and Henschel 2-6-4T No. 088 of 1929 on shed at Contumil in August 1972.

CP broad gauge Hartmann 0-4-0T No. 002, in steam and on shed at Contumil in August 1972. Built in 1881, this was the oldest steam locomotive in use on Portuguese Railways – ninety-one years old at the time of this photo.

CP broad gauge 2-8-0 No. 715, manufactured to the same design as the Schwartzkopf 710, but in a later batch built by North British in 1921, on shed at Contumil in August 1972.

CP broad gauge Beyer Peacock 0-6-2T No. 013, built in 1889, and 1912-built Schwartzkopf CP 2-8-0 No. 705, outside the 'new' roundhouse at Contumil in August 1972.

CP broad gauge Beyer Peacock 0-6-2T No. 014, built in Manchester in 1890, heads a line of dumped locomotives at Contumil in August 1972. This loco was subsequently restored and preserved.

CP broad gauge 2-8-4T No. 0185, built by Henschel in 1924, is seen at Lousado in August 1972. Ten of this class were originally built for service in the south but all were based at Contumil by the 1970s.

CP broad gauge 2-6-4T No. 072, built by Societe Suisse in 1916, takes on water en route from Lousado to Contumil in August 1972. These tanks were by far the most numerous of steam locomotives in Portugal.

Sernada do Vouga, former headquarters of the Val do Vouga (VV) railway and focal point for the 140-mile Vouga and Dao metre gauge systems. Trains for Espinho and Aveiro prepare to depart and the shed and works can be seen to the right in this view from August 1972.

Metre gauge Borsig 4-6-0T CP No. E122 and Henschel Mallet 2-4-6-0T CP No. E211 are prepared for service at Sernada do Vouga in August 1972.

CP metre gauge 2-6-0T engines Nos E94 and E95, built by Decauville in 1910, under repair in the former VV works at Sernada do Vouga in August 1972.

CP metre gauge 4-6-0T No. E122, one of four of a class built by Borsig for VV in 1908, is prepared for service at Sernada do Vouga in August 1972.

CP metre gauge 2-8-2T No. E131, one of a class of just three engines built by Henschel for the VV in 1924, waits at Espinho in August 1972.

CP metre gauge Henschel 2-4-6-0T Mallet No. E212, built in 1923, rests by the water tower at Espinho, the western terminus of the Linha do Vouga line, in August 1972.

A crowded metre gauge train leaves Espinho with a Vouga line train bound for Sernada in August 1972. At the front is Henschel 2-8-2T CP No. E131, backed up by Henschel 2-4-6-0T Mallet CP No. E212.

Kessler 2-6-0T CP No. E84 at Agueda station, August 1972. Built in 1886, and eighty-six years old at the time of this photo, this was one of the oldest steam locomotives still in use on the Portuguese railways.

The Douro valley in northern Portugal, the home of Port wine, runs 125 miles from Porto to the Spanish border at Barca d'Alva and in the 1970s was also home to a fantastic array of both broad and metre gauge locomotives.

Broad gauge 2-8-0 CP No. 719, built by North British in 1921, at Regua shed in August 1972. These 2-8-0s handled the bulk of steam-hauled freight traffic in Portugal.

Mixed gauge engines on shed at Regua in September 1974. Metre gauge 2-4-6-0T Mallets mix with broad gauge 4-6-0 engines. The photo was taken from my bedroom window in the Pensao Borges just across the street.

CP inside-cylinder broad gauge 4-6-0 No. 286 on Regua shed in September 1974. This class of just six engines were built in 1910 by Henschel of Germany; they were nicknamed B12s due to their similarity with the Great Eastern Railway 4-6-0s.

Lots of activity is evident on Regua station as CP inside-cylinder broad gauge Henschel 4-6-0 No. 286 arrives with a train from Tua in August 1972.

Henschel metre gauge 0-4-0T CP No. E1, built in 1922, had been out of use since the late 1960s but is seen here in August 1972 looking recently ex-works and performing its duties as Regua station pilot.

CP metre gauge Henschel 2-4-6-0T Mallet No. E214, built in 1923, arrives at Regua with a mixed train from Chaves on the Linha do Corgo line in August 1972.

CP metre gauge Henschel 2-4-6-0T No. E207 departs Vila Real with a Corgo line train bound for Regua in September 1974. Eighteen of these engines were built between 1911 and 1923.

CP metre gauge Hohenzollern 0-6-0WT No. E41, built in 1904, at Pocinho in September 1974. Pocinho was the junction for the most easterly of the Douro valley metre gauge lines, the Linha do Sabor.

CP metre gauge half-cab 0-6-0T No. E54, originally built by Kessler in 1889 for the Dao line, on shunting duties at Pocinho in September 1974.

CP broad gauge outside-cylinder Henschel 4-6-0 No. 292 and metre gauge Mallet 2-4-6-0T No. E216 being serviced at the mixed gauge shed at Pocinho in September 1974.

CP inside-cylinder broad gauge 4-6-0 No. 282, built by Henschel in 1910, waits at Pocinho with a mixed train in September 1974.

CP broad gauge outside-cylinder Henschel 4-6-0s Nos 291 and 292 and inside cylinder No. 282 at Pocinho in September 1974.

CP broad gauge outside-cylinder 4-6-0 No. 292, built by Henschel in 1913, arrives at Pocinho with a mixed train from Regua in September 1974.

CP broad gauge outside-cylinder 4-6-0 No. 294, built by Henschel in 1913, arriving at Pocinho with a mixed train in September 1974. I subsequently boarded this train for the onward journey to Barca d'Alva and the Spanish border.

CP broad gauge outside-cylinder 4-6-0 No. 291, built by Henschel in 1913, leaving Pocinho with a mixed train bound for Regua in September 1974.

Spain

The Spanish National Railways (RENFE) 141F 2-8-2 'Mikados' were built between 1953 and 1960. Here, in August 1974, 141F No. 2324 prepares to depart Alsasua, in north-east Spain, with a mixed freight.

RENFE Class 141F 2-8-2 No. 2221 at Castejon de Ebro station in August 1974. Twenty-five Mikados were originally ordered from North British (Nos 2101–125). The Scottish company then delivered another batch of 100 disassembled units (Nos 2201–300) for assembly in Spain.

RENFE 141Fs Nos 2362 and 2369 on shed at Alsasua in August 1974. A final batch of 117 Mikado locomotives (Nos 2301–417) were built entirely in Spain by MTM, Babcock & Wilcox, Euskalduna and Macosa.

RENFE Class 141F 2-8-2 No. 2362 on shed and in steam at Alsasua in August 1974. At the time of this picture, the 141Fs had become the last active RENFE steam locomotives in Spain.

RENFE Class 141F 2-8-2 No. 2417 leaving Castejon with the 09.28 passenger working to Alsasua in August 1974. Castejon was a busy junction serving Miranda and Alsasua to the north, Zaragoza to the south and Soria to the west.

RENFE Class 141F 2-8-2 No. 2221 departs Castejon with a freight bound for Zaragoza. Six hours spent at Castejon on 27 August 1974 yielded seventeen freight workings, of which nine were 141F steam-hauled.

RENFE Class 141F 2-8-2 No. 2318 arrives at Castejon with a freight from Soria in August 1974. The same engine returned to Soria about three hours later.

RENFE Class 141F 2-8-2s Nos 2273 and 2210, both part of the batch delivered by North British for assembly in Spain, simmering in the midday heat at Castejon in August 1974.

A general view of the shed at Castejon shed as RENFE 141F No. 2221 is prepared for duty in August 1974. Castejon was one of the last outposts of Spanish steam; the shed here closed just eight months later, in April 1975.

RENFE Class 141F 2-8-2s Nos 2215, 2318, 2262, 2369 and 2315 in the roundhouse at Castejon in August 1974.

A wider view of the roundhouse and 141Fs at Castejon in August 1974. Twenty-seven 141Fs could be found on shed on this day in August 1974, though only six were in steam and ready for work.

RENFE Class 141F 2-8-2 No. 2221 taking on water at Castejon shed in August 1974. The engine later departed with a freight bound for Zaragoza (see previous page).

A pair of RENFE 141Fs at Salamanca in August 1974. Note the single chimneys, which identify these locomotives as part of the North British-supplied batch, the later Spanish-built engines having a double exhaust.

RENFE Class 141F 2-8-2 at Salamanca shed in August 1974. Steam workings were few around Salamanca though there were six 141Fs on the shed that day, four in steam, and my train onward to Portugal was hauled by 141F No. 2259.

RENFE Class 141F 2-8-2 No. 2227 at Miranda de Ebro, August 1972. On the shed at Miranda that day were twenty-seven steam locomotives (fifteen 141Fs, eight 242Fs, three 241Fs and an 0-6-0 tank).

RENFE Class 141F 2-8-2 No. 2288 on shed at Miranda de Ebro in August 1974. Two years later and a similar number of engines could be found on shed, though only five of twenty 141Fs were in steam and the eight 242Fs had all been withdrawn.

By the summer of 1974 only the 141Fs remained in RENFE service. Here a 4-8-2 RENFE Class 241F, No. 4078, lies abandoned at Castejon in August 1974.

Giant oil-burning RENFE 4-8-4 Class 242F 'Confederation' No. 2003 on shed at Miranda de Ebro in August 1972. Ten of these locomotives were built in 1955/56 by Maquinista (MTM).

RENFE 242Fs on shed at Miranda de Ebro in August 1972. All ten locomotives of the class were assigned to Miranda de Ebro and spent their last years hauling freight on the Miranda–Castejon–Zaragoza–Alsasua line.

RENFE 242F No. 2008. By the time I returned to Miranda de Ebro in August 1974, the 242Fs were dumped out of use, many with their connecting rods cut.

The metre gauge Ponferrada–Villablino railway in north-western Spain was one of the last steam-operated railways in Western Europe. The line ran 40 miles from Ponferrada north into the mountainous region around Villablino. This is a general view over the shed at Ponferrada in August 1974.

The line was built in 1919, in just 10 and a half months, to carry coal from mines near Villablino to a power station at Cubillos, or to the RENFE network at Ponferrada. This is another general view over the shed at Ponferrada from August 1974.

PV No. 11, Krauss 2-6-0 No. 7626 of 1920, on shed at Ponferrada in August 1974. This engine was acquired second-hand in 1938 and was the first engine to arrive at the line after an initial batch of Baldwin 2-6-2Ts supplied in 1919.

A pair of 'Engerth' 2-6-0s, PV No. 31 (Maffei No. 3350 of 1913) and PV No. 17 (Krauss No. 6918 of 1914), at Ponferrada in August 1974. Although these locos look like conventional tender engines, the tender is actually mounted on the main frames by beams which rest on brackets behind the driving wheels to improve adhesion.

Broad gauge 0-6-0PT MSP No. 51, Haine St Pierre No. 1382 of 1922, shunting the RENFE exchange sidings at Ponferrada in August 1974.

PV No. 21, Borsig 2-6-0T No. 5032 of 1901, at Ponferrada in August 1974. This engine came to the line from the Sociedad Minera de Villaodrid (SMV) in June 1930 and spent the rest of its working life shunting around Ponferrada.

PV No. 10 *Villablino*, Baldwin 2-6-2T No. 52684 of 1919, at Ponferrada in August 1974. Ten of these tanks were built by Baldwin for the opening of the line and they handled all traffic until the first Krauss-Engerths arrived in the 1930s.

Another of the Baldwin 2-6-2Ts, PV No. 7 *Arana Lupardo*, Baldwin No. 52681 of 1919, at Ponferrada in August 1974. The Baldwins all carried brass cab-side plates with the names of people associated with the founding of the railway.

PV No. 13, Macosa 2-6-0 No. 101 of 1950, heads up the Sil valley with a train of empties bound for the mines at Villablino, Santa Marina, August 1974.

PV No. 11, Krauss 2-6-0 No. 7626 of 1920, brings a loaded coal train down the Sil valley from Villablino, Santa Marina, August 1974.

PV No. 17, Krauss 2-6-0 No. 6918 of 1914, crosses the River Sil at Santa Marina with a train of empties bound for the mines at Villablino in August 1974.

PV No. 15, Macosa 2-6-0 No. 150 of 1956, one of the last two engines to be delivered new to the PV, and one of the last Engerths to be built anywhere in the world, with a loaded coal train bound for Ponferrada at Santa Marina in August 1974.

PV No. 13, Macosa 2-6-0 No. 101 of 1950, lets off steam at Ponferrada in August 1974. The Macosa Engerths, PV Nos 13–16 were the only narrow gauge engines built by Macosa, the only Engerths to be built in Spain.

PV No. 31, Maffei 2-6-0 No. 3350 of 1913, approaching Ponferrada in August 1974. The oldest of the 2-6-0+4 Engerths, No. 31 was originally built for the Pamplona–San Sebastian railways and was bought by the PV in 1943.

PV No. 31, Maffei 2-6-0 No. 3350 of 1913, at Santa Marina in August 1974. For many years No. 31 was the preferred engine for the daily passenger train, though by the end of 1980 the 'correo' had stopped running and she was hauling coal instead.

PV No. 31, Maffei 2-6-0 No. 3350 of 1913, at Ponferrada passenger terminus in August 1974.

France

French National Railways (SNCF) Class 141R 2-8-2 No. 1132, built by Alco, on shed at Narbonne, August 1972. SNCF suffered incredible damage in the Second World War with around 80 per cent of locomotives destroyed or unserviceable at the end of the war.

An SNCF Class 141R 2-8-2 with a parcels train at Narbonne in August 1972. 1,340 141Rs were shipped to France between 1945 and 1947. Most were built in the US though 140 came from Canada. They were the last type in active service in France.

SNCF Class 141TB 2-8-2T No. 460 shunting at Provins, France, in August 1972. The 141TBs were originally a series of 112 engines built for the Est Railway between 1910 and 1917. They were the most numerous tank locomotives of the Est Railway and spent much of their life handling suburban services out of Paris.

In 1969, following the end of steam on Paris eastern suburban services, the 141TBs were transferred to various provincial lines. Some, such as that pictured here, were leased to the CFTA network of Provins and survived until shortly after this picture was taken in August 1972.

Italy

The Italian State Railways (FS) shed at Cremona, in the Lombardy region of northern Italy, featured over twenty locomotives of Classes 625, 685, 740, 741, 743, 835 and 880 at the time of my visit in August 1974.

FS Class 625 2-6-0 No. 625.118 leaving Cremona in August 1974. 108 of this class were built by various companies in Italy between 1910 and 1914 and a further eighty constructed between 1922 and 1923. The gap in production was caused by the First World War.

FS Class 625 2-6-0 No. 625.116 leaves Piadena, a busy junction at the crossroads of the Cremona to Mantova and Parma to Brescia lines, in August 1974. The Class 625 locomotives were designed for mixed traffic operation and were designed to work on steep gradients.

FS Class 625 2-6-0 No. 625.011 at Venice Santa Lucia in August 1974. The 625s were withdrawn from main line service in 1976, though a number were mothballed in working condition until final withdrawal in 1998.

FS Class 640 2-6-0 No. 640.037 arrives at Pavia with empty coaching stock in August 1974. 173 inside-cylindered locomotives of this class were built between 1907 and 1930.

FS Class 640 2-6-0 No. 640.037 waits to depart Pavia with a train bound for Alessandria in August 1974. Originally built for pulling the principal express trains on Italian main lines, the 640s were soon replaced on these services by more powerful Class 680 and 685 2-6-2s.

FS Class 640 2-6-0 No. 640.036 with some ancient passenger coaching stock at Novara in August 1972. The 640s were soon relegated to pulling passenger trains on secondary lines with level ground.

FS Class 640 2-6-0 No. 640.003 at Alessandria in August 1974. This picture clearly illustrates the unusual three-axle tender that was fitted to all of the Class 640 locomotives.

FS Class 740 2-8-0 No. 740.246 on shed at Cremona in August 1972. The first Class 740 locomotives were built in 1911 and production continued until 1923, albeit with a long interruption caused by the First World War.

FS Class 740 2-8-0 No. 740.246 at Piadena in August 1974. 470 of the 740s were built, making them the most numerous steam locomotive on the FS.

FS Class 740 2-8-0 No. 740.282 on shed at Alessandria in August 1974. Built for heavy freight work, the Class 740 saw service on the whole FS network; they were also employed for passenger services on secondary lines.

A very clean FS Class 740 2-8-0 No. 740.455, used on cross-border trains into Yugoslavia, at Nova Gorica in August 1974. In the 1940s and 1950s many of the class were fitted with Franco-Crosti boilers and reclassified as Class 741 and 743.

FS Class 743 Franco-Crosti boilered 2-8-0 No. 743.283 shunting at Piadena in August 1974. The addition of the Franco-Crosti boiler delivered a 10 per cent saving in coal consumption and was made to existing Class 740s at Verona works.

FS Class 743 Franco-Crosti boilered 2-8-0 No. 743.398 on shed at Cremona, August 1974. Ninety-five of the 740 class were so converted between 1941 and 1953.

FS Class 743 Franco-Crosti boilered 2-8-0 No. 743.283 arriving at Piadena in August 1974. This picture clearly illustrates the two preheater barrels, placed either side of the boiler, that were characteristic of the Franco-Crosti conversion.

FS Class 741 Franco-Crosti boilered 2-8-0 No. 741.137 at Cremona in August 1974. The Class 741, also rebuilt from Class 740s, was distinguished by a single preheater barrel and single chimney, placed on the right side of the locomotive.

FS Class 835 0-6-0T No. 835.240, station pilot at Alessandria in August 1974. 370 of the class were built by various Italian builders between 1906 and 1922 and became the standard steam shunter of the FS.

FS Class 835 0-6-0T No. 835.231 shunting at Udine in August 1974. These locomotives spent their careers on shunting duties throughout all the Italian network.

FS Class 835 0-6-0T No. 835.014 at Verona Porta Nuova station in August 1974. The first ninety-seven locomotives, which included the one shown here, were built by Ernesto Breda between 1906 and 1908.

FS Class 835 0-6-0T No. 835.014 at Verona Porta Nuova station in August 1974. The 835s soldiered on until the end of steam in Italy with some thirty locomotives still active in the early 1980s.

FS Class 880 2-6-0T No. 880.108 at Udine in August 1974. The Class 880 class was designed for use on secondary lines and was an evolution of the earlier FS Class 875. It was built 1912–22.

FS Class 880 2-6-0T No. 880.200 on shed at Cremona in August 1974. Sixty locomotives of the class were originally built between 1916 and 1922.

FS Class 880 2-6-0T No. 880.027 at Bra in August 1974. A further 115 Class 880s were derived from a rebuild of Class 875 locomotives between 1931 and 1933.

FS Class 880 2-6-0T No. 880.054 at Cremona in August 1974. The 880s were very suitable for service on flat lines hauling passenger and freight trains with a modest number of wagons.

A pair of FS Class 940 2-8-2Ts, Nos 940.030 and 940.028, at Pistoia in September 1974. A total of fifty-three locomotives of the class were built in Italy between 1922 and 1924.

FS Class 940 2-8-2T No. 940.027 at Pistoia in September 1974. The class was originally designed to handle the steep gradients of the Apennine mountain railways and was adapted from the Class 740 design.

FS Class 940 2-8-2T No. 940.015 at Villazzano, near Trento, in August 1974. The 940s have identical boilers, cylinders and wheels to the Class 740 locomotives.

FS Class 940 2-8-2T No. 940.015 at Villazzano, near Trento, in August 1974. Locomotives of the class remained in service until the end of regular steam services on the FS network.

Austria

An Austrian State Railways (OBB) Class 77 4-6-2T and Class 78 4-6-4T on shed and awaiting duty at Vienna Nord in August 1972. Both locomotives are fitted with a Giesl ejector, invented by Austrian engineer Dr Adolph Giesl-Gieslingen to increase power and reduce coal consumption.

An OBB Class 77 4-6-2T departs Vienna Praterstern in August 1972. A hundred of the Class 77s were built in several batches between 1913 and 1928; intended for light express passenger trains, they were ideal for the Vienna suburban services.

An OBB Class 78 4-6-4T departs Vienna Praterstern in August 1972. The Class 78s were built in Austria between 1931 and 1939 and were designed for hauling light fast trains over short distances.

An OBB Class 77 4-6-2T departs Vienna Praterstern in August 1972. Four steam-hauled commuter trains left Praterstern each evening for the towns of Retz and Bernhardstahl on the Czech border, returning the following morning.

OBB Class 93 2-8-2Ts at Schwarzenau in northern Austria in September 1974. These standard 2-8-2Ts were introduced in 1927 for secondary line services and became the most numerous tank locomotives in Austria.

OBB Class 93 2-8-2T No. 93-1418 departs Schwarzenau with a local passenger train for Martinsberg in September 1974. The Class 93s were all built in Austria by Lokomotivfabrik Floridsdorf.

OBB Class 93 2-8-2T No. 93-1432, acting as station pilot for the day, takes water at Schwarzenau in September 1974. Note the Giesl ejector that was fitted to the majority of the class.

A pair of OBB Class 93s, 93-1394 and 93-1418, at Schwarzenau in September 1974. By the 1970s, over half of the remaining class were allocated to Mistelbach for operating the network of secondary services north of Vienna.

The Waldviertel railway in north-east Austria is an 82-km network of 760 mm narrow gauge lines radiating from Gmund on the Czech border. The network was operated by the OBB from 1922. Here an OBB Class 399 0-8+4, No. 399.03, is in steam at Gmund in September 1974.

OBB 760 mm narrow gauge Class 298 0-6-2T No. 298.207 at Gmund in September 1974. This was one of three locomotives built in Linz, Austria, by Krauss in 1905.

OBB Class 399 0-8+4 No. 399.06, with a mixed train of mixed-gauge stock, at Gmund in September 1974. The Class 399 were 'Engerth' type locomotives – an articulated construction whereby the tender frames reach around the firebox and are linked to the engine behind the fourth driving axle.

Six Class 399s were originally built in 1906 for the Mariazell line in Lower Austria but were distributed to other narrow gauge railways following the electrification of that line in 1911. All have been subsequently preserved.

The Erzbergbahn or 'Iron Mountain railway' is a standard gauge rack and adhesion line built to convey iron ore from the Erzberg mountain to a steelworks at Donawitz, some 20 miles away. Here, OBB Class 97 0-6-2T No. 97-208 languishes on shed at Vordernberg in September 1974.

A regular passenger service also ran up the mountain from Vordernberg to Eisenerz. Eighteen of these Class 97 four-cylinder rack and adhesion engines were built in Austria between 1890 and 1908.

A pair of Class 97s start the 5½-mile 1 in 14 climb out of Vordernberg to the summit at Prabichl whilst another pair can be seen down in the station at Vordernberg.

Another pair of Class 97s tackle the mountain. These engines each have two separate two-cylinder engines, one set driving the adhesion wheels and the other the cogged rack wheels.

The Graz-Koflacher Bahn (GKB) is a 92-km network of railways in Styria, Austria, originally opened in 1873 to serve the coal mines of the area. Here, ex-OBB 2-10-0 'Kriegslok' No. 152-1367 is seen at Graz in September 1974.

Ex-OBB 2-10-0 Class 52 'Kriegslok' No. 152-3110 arrives tender-first at Graz with a freight in September 1974. The Class 52s were a wartime development of the pre-war Class 50 (opposite page), using fewer parts and cheaper materials to speed production. They became the most numerous steam locomotive type in the world.

Ex-OBB Class 50 2-10-0 No. 50-685 departs Graz with a mixed freight on the Graz-Koflacher Bahn in September 1974. The Class 50s were built by the German Reichsbahn (DRG) from 1939 as a standard class freight engine.

Ex-OBB Class 50 2-10-0 No. 50-685 at the coaling stage at Graz shed in September 1974. This locomotive was originally bought from the OBB for the GKB in 1972 before being sold into preservation in 1978.

Ex-OBB Class 56 2-8-0 No. 56-3297 on the Graz-Koflacher Bahn at Graz in September 1974. The Class 56 locomotives were originally built in Austria between 1897 and 1919 and were the mainstay of freight traffic in the First World War.

This ornate 0-6-0 tender locomotive, No. 671, was originally built in Austria in 1860 for the Austrian Southern Railway. It came to the GKB in 1920; it was never withdrawn and remains the oldest continuously operating locomotive in the world. It has been preserved and is frequently on duty to haul steam specials today.

OBB Class 52 2-10-0 'Kriegslok' No. 52-3816 moves off the shed at Linz in August 1972. There was plenty of steam on shed at Linz at this time, mainly Class 52s and Class 77 4-6-2Ts – their duties being mainly on the line north to the Czech border at Summerau and south towards Selzthal.

Another view of OBB Class 52 2-10-0 'Kriegslok' No. 52-3816 at Linz. This one also has a 'Kabintender' which was added to the Class 52s to provide accommodation for guards and dispensed with the need for a separate van.

West Germany

German Federal Railways (DB) Class 012 oil-fired two-cylinder 4-6-2 'Pacific' No. 012-081 at Aschendorf, near Rheine, in May 1975. Fifty-five of these three-cylinder Pacifics were built by Schwartzkopf during the war and were put to work on the fastest and heaviest expresses.

A DB Class 012 4-6-2 Pacific near Rheine in May 1975. After the Second World War the entire class was retired and remained sidelined until 1949, when they were completely refurbished.

DB Class 012 4-6-2 No. 012-063 at Hilter, near Rheine, in May 1975. Originally classified as 01¹⁰, many were converted to oil-burning in the 1950s and became DB Class 012; those that remained as coal burners were classified 011.

DB Class 012-100 at Hilter, on the Rheine–Emden line, in May 1975. These locomotives had a top speed of 150 km/h and were capable of hauling 500 tonnes at 120 km/h.

DB Class 001 two-cylinder coal-fired 'Pacific' No. 001-173, built by Henschel in 1936, at Hof in August 1972. These Class 01 locomotives were the first production series standard express train locomotives of the Deutsche Reichsbahn.

Class 01[10] was a development of the Class 01s. Here, one of the very last DB Class 01[10] three-cylinder coal-fired 4-6-2 'Pacifics', No. 011-072, is on the turntable at Rheine in August 1972.

DB Class 023 2-6-2 No. 023-002 on shed at Crailsheim in September 1974. The Class 023s were constructed between 1950 and 1959 and were the last main line steam locomotives to be built in Germany.

DB Class 023 2-6-2 No. 023-005 at Crailsheim in September 1974. 105 of the class were built, by four different builders, to fill a need for medium-sized mixed traffic locomotives.

The Prussian State Railways Class P8 (DB Class 38) was a 4-6-0 locomotive built from 1906 to 1923 by the Berliner Maschinenbau (previously Schwartzkopf) and twelve other German factories. Here DB No. 038-772 is seen on shed at Rottweil in August 1972.

3,850 of these fine engines were built and eventually distributed all over Europe as war reparations. In West Germany they ended their days in the Stuttgart area in the early 1970s. Here, DB No. 038-382 is seen at Tubingen in August 1972.

These ex-Prussian Class G8 locomotives were eight-coupled superheated freight locomotives. They were built from 1902 to 1921 by various German manufacturers and eventually became Class 055 of the DB. These examples were seen out of use at Köln Gremberg shed in August 1972.

A very rusty DB Class 055 0-8-0 (formerly a Prussian G8), dumped at Lingen in August 1972. Over 6,000 G8 and G8.1 locomotives were built and were distributed all over Europe following the Second World War.

DB Class 042 2-8-2 No. 042-266 with a northbound freight at Hilter, on the Rheine–Emden line in May 1975. Introduced in 1936, the Class 42s were intended as fast goods train locomotives.

DB Class 042 2-8-2 No. 042-364 at Lehe, on the Rheine–Emden line, in May 1975. 366 of these standard engines had been built by Schwartzkopf by 1941 and classified 41 by the DRB though further building of the class was cancelled with the advent of the Second World War.

DB Class 042 2-8-2 No. 042-164 at Hilter, on the Rheine–Emden line, in May 1975. Originally built as coal-burners, some were converted to oil-burning by the DB and reclassified 042.

DB Class 042 2-8-2 No. 042-186 at Fresenburg, on the Rheine–Emden line, in May 1975. The Class 042s survived until the very last day of steam on the Deutsche Bundesbahn in October 1977.

An oil-fired variant of the DRG Class 44 2-10-0 heavy goods locomotive, DB No. 043-100 is seen with an empty car transporter freight at Lehe on the Rheine–Emden line in May 1975.

Oil-fired DB Class 043 2-10-0 No. 043-085 heading northbound with a long train of empty ore wagons at Tinnen, on the Rheine–Emden line, in May 1975.

Oil-fired DB Class 043 2-10-0 No. 043-737 on shed at Rheine in May 1975. These locomotives were built in huge numbers from 1937; conversion to oil-firing started in 1955.

Two DB Class 044 2-10-0s, oil-fired No. 043-666 and coal-fired No. 044-180, double-head a heavy ore freight near Rheine in May 1975. The Class 44s were by far the most powerful locomotives in Germany.

DB Class 044 2-10-0 heavy goods locomotive No. 044-553 arrives at Gelsenkirchen in the Ruhr on a murky afternoon in August 1972.

DB Class 044 2-10-0 No. 044-534 hauls a heavy-laden ore train bound for the Ruhr at Devermuhlen on the Rheine–Emden line in May 1975. The Class 44s were capable of hauling 2,000-ton trains on level track at 35 mph.

DB Class 44s on shed at Wanne-Eickel in the Ruhr on 25 May 1975. Over twenty 2-10-0s of Class 50 and 44 could be found on shed that day.

DB Class 044 2-10-0 No. 044-552 silhouetted against an early evening sky as it heads northbound, light engine, near Leer on the Rheine–Emden line in May 1975.

DRB Class 50 2-10-0s were procured as part of Germany's war preparations and were built from 1939 as a standard locomotive for hauling goods trains. Here, several DB Class 50s are seen on shed at Dillingen in August 1972.

The Deutsche Bundesbahn grouped the locomotives into Classes 050, 051, 052 and 053 from 1968 for computer compatibility. Here, No. 052-406 is seen at Crailsheim in September 1974.

The Class 50s became a universal class of mixed traffic engine and could be found in the 1970s performing a wide range of duties. DB Class 50 Nos 051-414 and 052-239 are seen on shed at Kaiserslautern in August 1972.

By the 1970s Class 50s could be commonly seen on passenger workings, as with this example, No. 052-481, which had just arrived at Crailsheim with a train from Aalen in September 1974.

DB Class 064 2-6-2T No. 064-305 passes the works at Aschaffenburg in August 1972. 520 Class 64s were built by various manufacturers between 1928 and 1940.

DB Class 81 0-8-0T No. 081-004 stored for future preservation at Bochum Dallhausen in May 1975. The Class 81s were intended as a standard goods tank locomotive, though just ten were built and delivered by Hanomag in 1928.

DB Class 82 0-10-0T No. 082-008, newly painted and destined for preservation, at Lingen works in August 1972. Forty-one of the class were built by Henschel, Krupp and Esslingen between 1950 and 1955 and primarily deployed in the marshalling yards of north-west Germany.

DB Class 86 2-8-2T No. 086-407 at Hof in August 1972. The Class 86 was a standard goods train tank locomotive intended for use on branch lines. 775 of the class were built between 1928 and 1943.

DB Class 078 4-6-4T No. 078-453 ready for duty at Rottweil in August 1972. Originally Prussian Class T18, almost 500 were built between 1912 and 1927 by the Vulkan Naval Yards at Stettin.

One of the last surviving DB Class 078 4-6-4Ts, No. 078-246, shunting 'silverfish' coaches at Rottweil in September 1974.

DB Class 94 0-10-0T No. 094-207 at Hamm shed in August 1972. The Class 94s were originally built as Class T16.1 goods train tank locomotives for Prussian State Railways between 1913 and 1924.

DB Class 94 0-10-0T No. 094-561 shunting at Emden in August 1972. 1,242 were built by various German manufacturers and deployed on heavy shunting and line duties throughout Germany.

A general view over the busy shed at Ehrang, Trier. Forty 2-10-0 steam locomotives of classes 044 and 050, and a solitary Class 023 2-6-2, were on shed on this day in August 1972.

On shed at Rottweil in September 1974: Prussian P8 DB Class 038 4-6-0 No. 038-383, Prussian T18 DB Class 078 4-6-4T No. 078-246 and DB Class 50 2-10-0 No. 050-383.

'Letzte Fahrt mit Dampf' – DB Class 012 4-6-2 'Pacific' No' 012-066 makes a last run at Lingen in May 1975. The Class 012s were finally withdrawn from service on 31 May 1975.

'Dampflok Abschied' – DB Class 042 2-8-2 No. 042-096 prepares to depart Rheine with an 'end of steam' special on 10 September 1977. Main line steam on the Deutsche Bundesbahn ended on 26 October 1977 with the very last movement of Class 043 2-10-0 No. 043-196.

Eastern Europe

East German (DR) 'Reko' Class 01.5 oil-fired 4-6-2 'Pacific' No. 01-0502 pauses at Buchen with a cross-border express from Hamburg in August 1972. This locomotive was one of thirty-five Class 01s rebuilt at Meiningen in 1962.

DR Class 50.35 'Reko' 2-10-0 No. 50-3639 at Wernigerode in August 1977. These locomotives were rebuilds ('Rekoloks') of the standard Class 50 and received a longer boiler and various other improvements aimed at raising performance.

DR Class 50.35 'Reko' 2-10-0 No. 50-3645 at Wernigerode in August 1977. 208 such Class 50s were rebuilt between 1958 and 1962.

DR Class 50.35 'Reko' 2-10-0 No. 50-3708 at Wernigerode in August 1977. This class survived until the very end of standard gauge steam in East Germany in 1988.

The engines of DR Class 99.23 are metre gauge 2-10-2T steam locomotives that were procured by the Deutsche Reichsbahn from 1954 to 1956. Here DR No. 99-0236 departs Drei Annen Hohne in October 1978.

DR Class 99.23 oil-fired 2-10-2T No. 99-0245. These engines were converted to oil-burning between 1976 and 1981, and renumbered to 02xx from 72xx, a change that did not last long as they were converted back to coal between 1982 and 1984.

DR Class 99.23 oil-fired 2-10-2T No. 99-0236 on shed at Wernigerode in October 1978. The Class 99.23 were the most powerful German narrow gauge steam locomotives ever to have been built.

DR Class 99.23 coal-fired 2-10-2T No. 99-7239 shunting freight wagons at Hasserode in October 1978. These magnificent engines are all now owned and run on the 140 km network of the Harzer Schmalspur Bahnen (HSB).

Yugoslavian State Railways (JZ) Class 36 2-10-0 No. 36-048 at Nova Gorica in August 1974. Forty-nine of these locomotives, former Prussian G12s, were handed over from Germany as war reparations at the end of the Second World War.

Yugoslavian (JZ) No. 36-048 at the coaling stage at Nova Gorica in August 1974. These three-cylinder 2-10-0s were among the most powerful freight engines in Yugoslavia and were well-suited to hauling freight over the steeply graded route between Jesenice and Sezana.

Yugoslavian (JZ) Class 17 2-6-2T No. 17-020 at Nova Gorica, Yugoslavia, in August 1974. The Class 17s were originally Hungarian Class 342s and came to Yugoslavia following the break-up of the Austrian Empire.

Yugoslavian (JZ) Class 06 2-8-2 No. 06-002 at Spielfeld Strass in September 1974. These 'standard' mixed traffic locomotives were built by Borsig in Germany in 1930.

Czech (CSD) Class 556 2-10-0 No. 556.0506 sporting symbols of communist Czechoslovakia. This locomotive crossed the Iron Curtain border from Ceske Velenice to Gmund, Austria, several times a day with both freight and passenger workings.

Czech (CSD) Class 556 2-10-0 No. 556.0506 returns across the border to Ceske Velenice in September 1974. The Class 556s were powerful 2-10-0 freight locomotives and Skoda built 510 examples up to 1958.